Simply Romantic Ideas

150 Fun and Creative Ways to Romance Your Husband

Honor Books
Tulsa, Oklahoma

All scripture quotations are taken from the *New American Standard Bible*. Copyright ©
The Lockman Foundation 1960, 1962, 1963, 1968, 1971, 1972, 1973, 1975, 1977.
Used by permission.

3rd Printing

Simply Romantic Ideas:
150 Fun and Creative Ways to Romance Your Husband
ISBN 1-56292-448-6
Copyright ©1998 by Campus Crusade for Christ, Inc.
doing business as FamilyLife
3900 N. Rodney Parham Road
Little Rock, AR 72212

Published by Honor Books
P.O. Box 55388
Tulsa, OK 74155

Compiled and edited by Leslie J. Barner.

$\mathscr{F}$ o r e w o r d

What would your husband do if you looked him in the eye one night and asked, "Sweetheart, what can I do to let you know that I love you?" Or if you gave him a massage by candlelight? What would he think if you surprised him with a romantic weekend getaway . . . just the two of you? These ideas and more are included in this little book, to help you create a more romantic marriage!

Romance is not the foundation of marriage, but it is the fire in the fireplace of a relationship—the warmth and security that says, "We may have struggles, but I love you, and everything is okay." Romance also says, "Because I love you, I like pleasing you." Romantic love brings delight to your mate, making him feel special and important. It can return the enchantment and thrill of when you were dating, and give your own worth, in his eyes, an extra boost.

The FamilyLife speaker team has provided you with some of their best romance-building ideas—tried and proven in their own homes. Take them and adapt them to your own circumstances and personalities. Use them to spark some creativity of your own! Find out what your mate really likes, what things *he* considers romantic. Most of all, commit to doing those things that will make him feel more loved, appreciated, and valued. Like any good fire in the fireplace, marriage needs attention and fuel. So if romance is missing in your marriage, this book can help you ignite the fire! And if romance is already a regular part of your relationship, use it to fan the flames.

Dennis and Barbara Rainey
Dennis Rainey is the executive director of FamilyLife and father of six.
Barbara Rainey is co-founder of FamilyLife and mother of six.

Ways to Romance Your Husband:

Questions to Stimulate Intimate Conversations

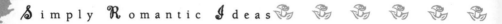

1.

What are five of the

most romantic things

I could ever do for you?

2.

What are the three most romantic times we've had together?

3.

H ow are we doing at keeping our marriage a priority? How are we communicating that to our children?

4.

Do we demonstrate our love for one another in front of our children on a regular basis?

5.

What are we teaching our children about marriage by our example?

6.

If walls could talk,

what would ours say?

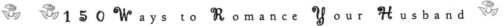
7.

In what ways

can we improve or

simplify our lifestyle?

8.

How should we celebrate our 25th

(or any milestone) anniversary?

What plans can we implement now

to make it a reality?

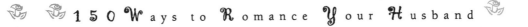
9.

What are our dreams and
goals for our marriage over
the next five years,
ten years, and beyond?

10.

$\mathcal{I}$f we had two days alone together,

what would be your idea of

how best to invest them?

11.

If you could go anywhere in the world,

where would you go, and why?

12.

Are you satisfied with our level

of intimacy? What could

we do to improve?

13.

What could I do to best help

you in the next 30 days?

14.

If you could change anything about the way I treat you, what would it be?

15.

When we make love, what do you enjoy most?

16.

What do I do that really makes you feel loved? What can I do to make you feel more loved?

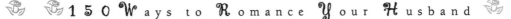

17.

Tell me about a time

when you felt really close to me.

What made you feel that way?

18.

If I could help you

fulfill your wildest dream,

what would you want me to do?

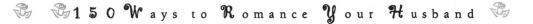

19.

What three things do you like

doing with me the most?

20.

$\mathscr{W}$ hat kind of clothing

(slacks, dress, skirt, suit, etc.)

do you most like to

see me wear, and why?

21.

What perfume do you most like for me to wear, and why?

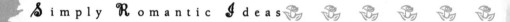
22.

If I were a car, what kind

would I be? Why?

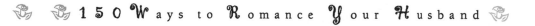
23.

What has God been

teaching you lately?

24.

What friend has most

influenced your life, how? `

25.

What do you want our family

to be remembered for?

26.

How am I doing at motherhood?

In what ways can I improve?

27.

How are we doing at providing loving discipline for our children? How can we do better?

28.

*I*n what ways do you think our
parents' marriages and parenting
techniques affect the marriage
we share and the parenting
techniques we use today?

29.

*L*ook back at your

childhood or teenage years.

What do you miss doing the most?

30.

What practical things could I do

to make your first few minutes

at home each evening more

relaxing and enjoyable?

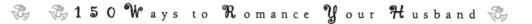

31.

Do you feel like you are the

"king of your castle"?

What can I do differently

to make you feel more that way?

32.

What can I do to help
you be the best husband
and father you can be?

Ways to Romance Your Husband:

Romantic Gestures

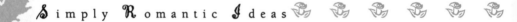

33.

Write an "I love you, _____"

message to your husband in

some creative way—like

in the snow or sand.

34.

Order pizza, turn the television set

to a game he wants to watch, and sit

with him. (Try to show genuine interest!)

If there's no game on, rent his

favorite adventure movie.

35.

$\mathscr{T}$hink of something God is teaching
you through your husband's leadership.
When he's not busy, go to him and
tell him what you're learning.

36.

Talk about how special he is

in front of others.

37.

Offer to help him with a project

that's been hanging over him.

38.

Fix your husband's favorite snacks and relax with him by listening to some of his favorite music. Then before bed, give him a passionate kiss and tell him you love spending time with him.

39.

Bring him a refreshing drink while he's doing yard work. Bring two lawn chairs and encourage him to take a short break.

40.

$\mathcal{P}$hone his job after you know he's

left for the day and leave a simple

but romantic message telling him

why you appreciate him.

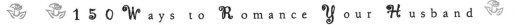

41.

On the fourth of July,

wake your husband early in the morning

and tell him you want to make

some fireworks of your own!

42.

Whatever your husband's favorite

activity (tennis, running, golf, bowling, etc.),

offer to participate with him.

If it's a game, try your best to learn

if you don't know how to play.

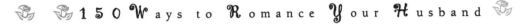

43.

Surprise him by

getting in bed naked

when he least expects it.

44.

$\mathscr{W}$ rite a poem for him or take the Song of Solomon 5:10-16 and rewrite portions, referring to his body using objects of nature to express your admiration of him ("Your shoulders are like the Sierra Mountains"). It's okay to laugh together as you read it to him!

45.

Identify an area in which your husband is strong or has really improved. Make him a card communicating your respect and admiration for him in this area.

46.

Mow the lawn for him.

(If you don't have a lawn,

take the trash out or do some

other job that is typically his.)

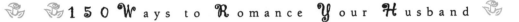

47.

Write five things you appreciate about your husband on five cards (one per card) and leave the cards in various places where he will find them.

48.

P ut a negligee or teddy in his

briefcase, gym bag, or lunch box

with a note telling him that you can't

wait for him to come home tonight!

49.

Before a business trip, fill his suitcase or briefcase with little treats (such as notes and surprises). Include one for every day that he's going to be away.

50.

F ix him a cup of coffee and

put it in his car with his

favorite donut or danish

for the ride to work.

51.

Make a button that says,
"I'm With My Hero."
Wear it some evening when
you are out with him.

52.

Surprise your husband one day

when he's taking a shower

and slip in with him.

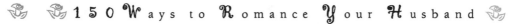

53.

Think of something that
your husband has asked
you to do and do it.

54.

*S*it close to him in church

and hold his hand.

55.

One Saturday morning, tell your husband that today he is "king for a day." Tell him he has no responsibilities that day except to enjoy himself. Ask him to design the perfect day. Take him someplace he enjoys, and prepare some of his favorite meals.

56.

$\mathcal{F}$ax your husband a love note.

Caution: be careful that it's not

too steamy! It might be a good

idea to include a cover page.

(Call him and ask him to go to the fax

machine so he is the only one who sees it.)

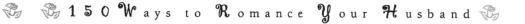
57.

Get up earlier than normal and fix your husband his favorite breakfast and serve it to him in bed.

58.

Once a week for the month

of December, send a Christmas

card to your husband at his office.

Include special messages of your own.

59.

Make up a coupon book
with coupons he can redeem
at any time. Examples: one free kiss,
one free back rub, breakfast in bed, help
in cleaning out his car, etc. Choose things
that he likes—things that would
communicate love to him!

60.

Give your husband a massage

with a nice body lotion or scented oil.

Be creative about what you wear.

61.

Go to his workplace after he has left work for the evening and decorate his office space with garland, balloons, and signs telling him you love him.

62.

While your husband is not around,

wash and wax his car and leave

him a love note with a single

red rose on the seat.

(You can hire a teenager to do the washing

and waxing if you don't think you're up to it.)

63.

Record a tape of love thoughts from you and put it in the cassette player of his car so it will play when he starts his car.

64.

Unexpectedly kiss

your husband on the back

of the neck or nibble his ear.

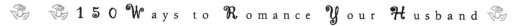

65.

Send a card with your husband

in the morning inviting him to

come home at lunch to enjoy

an intimate time together.

66.

While in public, discreetly play
with his hair, scratch his back,
rub his arm, or show him some
other kind of affection.

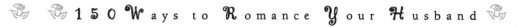

67.

Go with him to a computer, music,

or hardware store and encourage

him to buy himself something.

68.

$\mathcal{M}$ ake a special lunch for him
to take to work, or surprise him by
delivering lunch. Include special treats
and a coupon entitling him to a
romantic time when he gets home.

Ways to Romance Your Husband:

Ideas for Romantic Dates

69.

Get a sitter for the kids,

fix a candlelight dinner,

and meet your husband

at the door in lingerie.

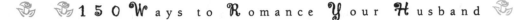

70.

Decorate the house in memory of
his favorite vacation spot, put on some
romantic music, and spend the evening
talking about special memories.

71.

For Valentine's Day,

fix a bubble bath and serve

his favorite snack or beverage

in the bathtub.

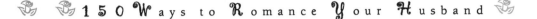

72.

Kidnap your husband from work,

if possible, (or early Saturday morning)

and spend the whole day doing things

he likes (fishing, ball game, etc.).

73.

Take your husband to a park
on a windy day and fly a kite.

74.

Just for fun, take your husband
to a sports car dealership and
go with him on some test drives.

75.

*P*repare a picnic dinner, pick your husband up from work, and take him to the beach, mountains, or a favorite scenic spot.

76.

$\mathcal{T}$ake your husband to a

go-cart track and race with him

(or take him bowling, miniature golfing, etc.).

77.

Take the kids to a sitter, unplug the phones, close the curtains, light the candles, lay a blanket down in the living room, and wait for him to come home for a special time together.

78.

Rent a limousine (or have a friend

drive you in a nice car), pick up

your husband at work and bring

him to a nice romantic dinner—

at a restaurant, at home (no kids),

or at a secluded spot.

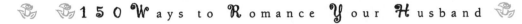

79.

Rent a romantic video and cuddle.

(Don't forget the popcorn!)

80.

Plan a romantic dinner at his

favorite restaurant, followed by

an unexpected overnight stay

at a local hotel, or friend's house

(while they are away).

81.

Take him on a shopping trip to Victoria's Secret and ask him to pick out an outfit he would like to see you in; then buy it and wear it that evening.

82.

Save up your quarters. Then one

evening, take your husband to the

nearest soda machine and announce

that you are going on a "quarter date"!

Go to places where you can spend

quarters, like an arcade. Be creative!

83.

Fix your husband a special meal and
serve it to him in bed. Wear something that
he would think is romantic, and decorate
the bedroom with candles and extra plants
(borrowed from other rooms in the house).
Make sure you arrange for the kids to be
away from home that evening.

84.

Take him on a progressive dinner at his favorite restaurants. For example: Mexican for appetizers, salad bar for salad, Italian for entrees, and cap it all off at a French café for dessert and coffee! (Hint: to avoid long waits, go on a night when business is usually slow.)

85.

Surprise him on a Saturday with
a picnic lunch at a lake or the beach and
spend the entire afternoon alone.

86.

Take him out for coffee and

dessert at an old-time cafe in

a nearby country town.

87.

Rent a room in a local hotel
for two or three hours
and have dinner via
room service.

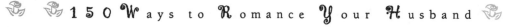

88.

Write him a love poem telling him

where you're taking him on a date;

then cut it up into puzzle pieces

and have him put it together.

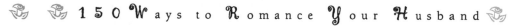

89.

Arrange to have a picnic lunch

or a candlelight dinner mid-field

at a local football stadium.

90.

Take the commuter train or city bus

to the city hot spot together for

dinner and an evening stroll.

91.

Cook dinner together, and

afterwards watch a movie.

92.

Take him to a football game

and have a tailgate supper

with one other special couple.

93.

Do something fun and
romantic that you did
when you were dating.

94.

Send him on a scavenger hunt

to find you at a romantic

dinner spot.

95.

Go to a wholesome comedy show,

and enjoy laughing your

socks off together!

96.

Take your husband to the

church where you were married

and have a picnic lunch on

the church steps or lawn.

(Remember to bring your wedding album.)

97.

Take two cameras and two new rolls of film to a special park, garden, beach, or zoo. Split up and see who can take the most interesting pictures. Meet back in one hour. Then, get the film processed at a one hour photo processing shop and discuss your photos over dinner at a restaurant.

98.

Start a collection of coupons for

restaurants and places to go. Then one

evening have a "coupon date night,"

using such coupons as, "Buy one dinner

get one free," "Miniature golf—

two for the price of one," etc.

Ways to Romance Your Husband:

Romantic Gift Ideas

99.

Buy him a new tie and surprise

him with it and a note saying,

"Just thinking of you."

100.

Buy some candy or other confection
that your husband enjoys. Wrap it in a
small box and place inside another
wrapped box; then put that box
in a bigger box and wrap it too.
Leave a note telling him,
"Deep down inside, you're a real sweetie!"

101.

*G*o to the store and buy him some

nice aftershave or cologne and leave

it in his car with a romantic card.

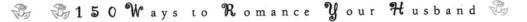

102.

Have his favorite pie delivered to
him at work with a special card.

103.

$\mathscr{P}$ resent him a "Journal of My Love
for You"—a journal that you fill
with dated love letters written to
your husband over a period of time.

104.

Buy your husband a
new shirt or tie and leave
it on his dresser with a card
telling him you love him
and are proud to be
his wife.

105.

Give him a card that acknowledges
his provision, leadership, strength,
courage, etc., especially when he
is in a stressful season at work.

106.

Get a picture of you and your husband (and kids if you'd like) and create a special card for him. Include a Scripture that you feel describes him.

(For example, Acts 11:24: "For he was a good man, and full of the Holy Spirit and of faith.")

107.

$\mathcal{G}$ o to your local florist,
pick up a rose, and leave it on
his windshield prior to the end of
the workday. If you'd like, attach
a passionate love note.

108.

Cut out cartoons from the newspaper
("Family Circle", "For Better or Worse", etc.)
that parallel your life together. Paste them
in a makeshift album, made from colored
construction paper. Write captions
explaining how the cartoon reminds
you of your marriage and family.
Be lighthearted and romantic.

109.

*B*uy a basket and fill it with

sweet things for your sweetheart

(for example: a note, honey, chocolate, jam,

a lollipop, heart-shaped candle, cologne, etc.)

110.

In the morning, give your husband a romantic card that contains your own passionate message expressing your desire for him; then fulfill the card that evening.

111.

Buy him tickets to a ball game
and place them in his Bible or
on the dashboard of his car.

112.

Put a bow on your head

and tell him to enjoy

unwrapping his present!

113.

Create a special Christmas tree ornament that describes, through words and/or pictures, why you appreciate your husband.

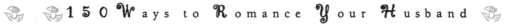

114.

Buy two of the same book by
his favorite author, and read them
simultaneously. Then have a "The End"
reading party together to discuss the book.

115.

G ive him a mini-tribute from you and

the kids, expressing in pictures

and writing how much you

love and appreciate him.

116.

Give him a collage with pictures of you together, representing your life over the years, with captions and brief notes about the collage.

117.

Give him a professional photograph

of yourself that is suitably

framed for his desk.

118.

Give him a hand-made
"Winner's Certificate" (like Publisher's
Clearing House) stating what he's won
and how he can redeem the prize.
The prize possibilities are limitless!

119.

B uy a book written by his

favorite author and read it

to him in bed each night.

120.

Give him a gift certificate to his favorite

store, and design a date using

what he buys with it.

121.

*G*ive him a photo album that contains

photos of special times and things

you've done together, with a

narrative under each picture.

122.

Give him a gift certificate
to a store where he can buy
something for his favorite
hobby (a sporting goods
store where he can buy
fishing gear, hunting gear,
golf supplies, etc.).

123.

Buy a small gift item

for one of his hobbies and

spend an afternoon with him

enjoying that hobby together.

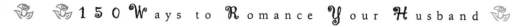

124.

Give him a gift certificate

to a massage therapist.

125.

Buy him a pair of silk boxers,

and present them with an

invitation to a night of passion.

126.

Buy tickets for two to his

favorite sporting event

for his birthday.

127.

Give him a gift certificate

for a car wash and wax.

128.

On a Friday morning,

give him a gift certificate

to a local coffee shop,

to be used together

on the weekend.

129.

Put together a small, but special,

travel toiletries kit for him to

use on a business trip.

130.

While your husband's on a

business trip, order room service

for him (pay by phone) to be served

as his wake-up call, with a special

yet simple love note from you.

131.

Buy him a nice but inexpensive time piece, with a note attached that says something like, "With every moment that passes in time, I fall more and more in love with you. . . ."

132.

On the last night of your husband's business trip, arrange for the hotel concierge to put a single rose by the bedside with a special note from you that says something romantic like, "I can't wait to see you again. . . ."

133.

Buy a "fun" ring for your

husband and give it to him

in a cracker-jack box.

134.

Buy a small gift (jewelry, fishing lure, etc.) and write down clues on paper, so that he has to solve the clues to find the gift.

135.

$\mathcal{G}$ ive him an envelope that contains

a check and an announcement

that says, "You've just won $50

(or whatever amount you choose)

to spend any way you want,

for being a wonderful husband!"

Ways to Romance Your Husband:

Romantic Getaways

136.

Surprise him with a romantic getaway at a bed-and-breakfast. Call him at work and tell him his bags are packed and where he should meet you.

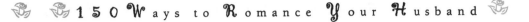

137.

Go on a scenic tour together

(a lighthouse tour, a covered bridge tour, etc.)

and create a romantic memory (like a kiss)

at each landmark along the way.

138.

Go on a romantic camping trip in a remote area where no one else would ever find you. Make sure there's a nice water hole for skinny dipping!

139.

Plan a surprise weekend getaway, giving him no details. Hide envelopes in the car (over sun visor, under seat, in glove compartment, under floor mat, etc.) with various clues that he can find on his way to the destination.

140.

$\mathcal{T}$ell him to meet you for dinner after work at a nice local hotel. Have bags already there in your room and dinner (delivered to your room just before he was supposed to meet you in the restaurant) with candlelight. Leave a note at the hotel restaurant for him to meet you in room #_____.

141.

After a romantic dinner, take him away (have bags packed and child care arrangements made in advance) to the nearest big city and spend the night in a classy hotel. The next day enjoy the sights and sounds of the city, heading home at sunset.

142.

P lan an overnight stay at a nice hotel
after one of his busiest weeks at work.
Bring your favorite take-out food with
you, and eat in those big fluffy robes,
then later, take a bath together and
spend the rest of the night cuddling.
Sleep in the next day, and wake him
with a light brunch and
a newspaper via room service.

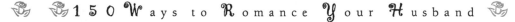

143.

Spend a weekend together on a

Christian work project or youth trip.

(It's surprising how it pulls you together.)

144.

*P*lan a surprise trip, beginning

with a pre-trip party to honor him,

then leave for the airport to fly

to your surprise destination.

145.

Charter a boat for

a weekend retreat.

(Remember to pack

his fishing gear!)

146.

Rent a log cabin in the mountains

for the weekend with a fireplace

and no phone or television.

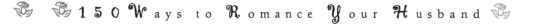

147.

Plan a weekend getaway at

a resort that specializes in

his favorite sport or hobby

(i.e. tennis courts, golf course, beach, etc.).

148.

Go on a mini ski vacation

in the mountains.

149.

*G*o on a canoe or rafting trip down
a lazy river. Stay in a cabin,
and enjoy the local fare.

150.

*K*idnap your husband from work. Have
his bags packed and head
for a surprise destination.

About the Authors...

The FamilyLife Marriage Conference speaker team is a dynamic, fun-filled group of people who are committed to encouraging and equipping couples to build strong marriages and godly homes. They are authors, teachers, ministers, executives, psychologists, marriage counselors, athletes, and business owners. They are also husbands, wives, fathers, and mothers—people just like you.

Though the speakers have varying backgrounds, each one has gained in-depth, real-life experience and education in the area of marriage and family.

At the FamilyLife Marriage Conferences, the speakers' presentations are biblically and professionally sound, and are designed to provide you with:

- Practical tools to strengthen and build your relationship

- Ways to open the channels of communication

- Creative methods to resolve conflict in your home

- Opportunities to bring you closer to your mate and your children

For many couples, the conference is a romantic getaway, or a time to draw closer to each other and to the Lord; for others it may help to save their marriage and family. But for all, the FamilyLife Marriage Conference is a "Weekend to Remember!"

If you would like more information on the FamilyLife Marriage or FamilyLife Parenting Conferences, please call 1-800-FL-TODAY.

The following couples comprise the speaker teams and were the contributors of these simply great ideas:

Barry & Pam Abell, Jose & Michelle Alvarez II, James & Anne Arkins, Bruce & Julie Boyd, Charles & Karen Boyd, Dan & Julie Brenton, Karl & Junanne Clauson, Doug & Patty Daily, Kyle & Sharon Dodd, Tim & Joy Downs, Don & Suzanne Dudgeon, Michael & Cindy Easley, Dennis & Jill Eenigenburg, Tom & Toni Fortson, Jerry & Nancy Foster, James & Cynthia Gorton, Floyd & Diana Green, Dick & Nancy Hastings, Howard & Jeanne Hendricks, David & Sharon Hersh, Bruce & Janet Hess, Alan & Theda Hlavka, Bob & Jan Horner, Joel & Cindy Housholder, Bill & Terri Howard, Don & Suzanne Hudson, Dan & Kathie Jarrell, Ron & Mary Jenson, Dave & Peggy Jones, Jim & Renee Keller, Tim & Darcy Kimmel, Bob & Mary Ann Lepine, Crawford & Karen Loritts, Ray & Robyn McKelvy, Tim & Noreen Muehlhoff, Bill & Pam Mutz, Johnny & Lezlyn Parker, Tom & Brenda Preston, Dick & Paula Purnell, Dennis & Barbara Rainey, Gary & Barbara Rosberg, Steve & Debbie Schall, Mark & Lisa Schatzman, Jeff & Brenda Schulte, Chuck & Beth Simmons, Greg & Bonnie Speck, Gary & Luci Stanley, Dave & Sande Sunde, Rick & Judy Taylor, Roger & Joanne Thompson, J.T. & Enid Walker, John & Linda Willett, Dave & Ann Wilson, Jerry & Sheryl Wunder, John & Susan Yates, Mick & Helen Yoder,

Special thanks to Lesie Barner for compiling and editing these ideas.

Additional copies of this book are available from your local bookstore.

Honor Books
Tulsa, Oklahoma